Original title:
Cosmic Karaoke Night

Copyright © 2025 Creative Arts Management OÜ
All rights reserved.

Author: Julian Montgomery
ISBN HARDBACK: 978-1-80567-858-8
ISBN PAPERBACK: 978-1-80567-979-0

Starbound Lyrical Journey

In a galaxy where rhymes take flight,
Aliens croon under the disco light.
A Martian sings with an out-of-tune slur,
While a comet taps dance, what a spectacular blur!

The robots are jiving, in circuits they groove,
A space cowgirl yodels, making the stars move.
Zany critters join with a howling refrain,
While asteroids rattle like a wild freight train!

Giggles erupt from a black hole's cheer,
As wormholes twist tunes that you just can't hear.
In this stellar bar, no one takes a seat,
With moonbeams as drinks, it can't be beat!

Supernova shouts cause a super fun blast,
While stardust confetti comes raining down fast.
So raise your voice high, don't hold back your glee,
In this strange universe, we're all wild and free!

Starstruck Solos

In spacesuits we croon, quite a sight,
With little green friends, we sing out of fright.
Asteroids dance to our off-key tunes,
While Saturn spins in its ringed cartoons.

Galaxies flash as we hit that high note,
An alien chokes on a floating remote.
We belt out ballads, and planets collide,
As comets join in, they can't run and hide.

Celestial Symphony

We gather near stars, under cosmic skies,
With lasers and lights, oh, how time flies!
A blue whale hums while the moon starts to sway,
Even Mars grins wide, in a Martian ballet.

Jupiter's thumps keep the rhythm in place,
While moons spin around, trying hard to keep pace.
We sing about aliens, our favorite pets,
And laugh as their faces turn from green to pets.

Melodies from the Multiverse

In a universe wide, we sing what we please,
With riffs from the stars that put us at ease.
Each parallel world has its own funky beat,
While time warps around us, we just can't be beat.

A unicorn waltzes on a rainbow line,
Sipping stardust sodas, feeling so fine.
We harmonize with comets, all glitter and glare,
As space dogs howl like they just don't care.

Echoes of Infinity

Echoes from black holes create a wild buzz,
As we sing of old tales, and how much it was.
Shooting stars join to make our chorus complete,
While nebulae wink, giving extra heartbeat.

From earth to the edges of every known sphere,
We giggle with laughter, each note bright and clear.
While quasars are twinkling, our voices take flight,
Making memories shine in the infinite night.

Odyssey of Voices

In the galaxy of karaoke, we sing,
With aliens jiving, it's quite the fling.
Moonbeams dance to a disco ball,
While meteorites crash, but we stand tall.

Stars twinkle in perfect tune,
As space cows moo under the moon.
Planets spin to our silly song,
In this cosmic party, we all belong.

Timeless Tunes

Jupiter's got jazz, Saturn's got soul,
Every single planet plays a role.
Neptune's on the mic, with a whale-like croon,
We all laugh and clap, to the bass of the moon.

Shooting stars join in, they frolic and play,
Galactic grooves that will never decay.
Each nebula laughs, says, 'Let's sing on repeat!'
These timeless tunes make us bounce on our feet.

Stellar Soundscapes

In the vastness of space, a tune so sweet,
A chorus of comets tap their feet.
The sun strums the rays, a guitar made of fire,
While black holes hum gently, never tire.

Planets hold hands, in a changing dance,
Aliens twirl in a whimsical trance.
Galaxies whirl in a jazzy display,
Making music together in the Milky Way.

Singing Supernova

A supernova bursts, what a sight to see,
Confetti of stars, a cosmic jamboree.
We're belting out ballads, no cares in the air,
With twinkling companions, joy everywhere.

The crowd of constellations chants with glee,
As comets join in, singing harmoniously.
We rhyme with the cosmos, wild and bizarre,
Under the shimmer of our favorite star.

Celestial Refrain

In the void, a mic shines bright,
Aliens sing with all their might.
Galactic tunes in zero G,
Even Mars joins in with glee.

Pluto's voice is quite a tease,
Singing softly, but with ease.
Saturn's rings dance in delight,
While stars twinkle, shining bright.

The Universe Unplugged

Black holes spin the latest hits,
While comets shake their little bits.
Nova lights flash, crowd goes wild,
Even asteroids groove, beguiled.

Jupiter's bass shakes all the moons,
As shooting stars play mellow tunes.
Venus glides with swishy flair,
Cosmic beings dance without a care.

Starlight Stage

A spaceship lands with flashy style,
Cosmic dancers go the extra mile.
Nebulas swirl in disco lights,
While meteorites take flight in sights.

Zodiac signs are in the zone,
Singing songs in deep monotone.
With asteroid belts as the floor,
Everyone chants, "We want more!"

Constellation Cadence

Big Dipper strums on a guitar,
Sirius shines, the brightest star.
Andromeda brings a high-pitched tune,
While Orion dances, howling at the moon.

Ursa Major leads a funky beat,
As planets gather, tapping their feet.
The Milky Way sways through the night,
In this cosmic fest of pure delight.

Celestial Riffs

Stars giggle and sway, under moonlight's embrace,
A comet's tail sings, with a sparkling grace.
Aliens groove, dance with their tentacle friends,
While Martians hum tunes, as the laughter transcends.

Planets spin jokes, in a clockwise parade,
Saturn's rings twirl, as the music is played.
Uranus pipes in, with a jester's delight,
Creating a symphony, under the night.

Skyward Serenades

Jupiter's bass drops, shakes the Milky Way,
While Venus chirps softly, in a shimmering sway.
Clouds turn to curtains, for this grand show,
Meteorites jive, as space breezes blow.

The sun strums a tune, on bright solar strings,
Blazing with laughter, as it warmly sings.
Echoes of joy bounce from faraway places,
As laughter ripples through celestial spaces.

Lunar Lullabies

The moon cracks a joke, in a silvery glow,
Craters rimmed with giggles, put on quite a show.
Stars whisper the punchlines, in playful delight,
As night wraps around us, with giggles so bright.

Asteroids bop, with a rhythm so neat,
Singing witty ballads on their winding beat.
Shooting stars blink, as if winking in jest,
Sharing cosmic tales, that leave us impressed.

Melodic Voyage

Rocketships launch into a symphony vast,
With alien choirs, singing songs of the past.
Nebulas twirl in their colorful dance,
While space-time unravels, in a cosmic romance.

Quasars pulse bright, keeping time with the fun,
As light-years drift by, and the laughter's begun.
Galactic giggles echo through the void,
In this joyous realm, where none feel annoyed.

Supernova Solos

In the void, a voice sang loud,
Stars blinked, forming a crowd.
Planets twirled in merry glee,
Jiving to tunes of space debris.

Aliens bobbed with neon pride,
Shooting stars twinkled, oh what a ride!
With harmonies that shook the night,
Galaxies grooved in pure delight.

Saturn spun with a swing and sway,
While black holes laughed their cares away.
Each supernova burst shared its sound,
As the universe twinkled all around.

From quasars high, the chorus soared,
In this theater, joy was stored.
Echoes danced in stellar delight,
Who knew the cosmos could be so bright?

Echoing Across the Cosmos

Take a seat on Mars' red dune,
Comets join in, singing a tune.
Neptune chuckled, shared a rhyme,
While Pluto grooved, though very mime.

Galactic winds carried the beat,
Stars in sync, they tapped their feet.
Asteroids rolled with laughter in tow,
Creating one epic cosmic show.

Sirius glowed, feeling the vibe,
Jupiter's moons joined in the tribe.
With every echo, laughter grew,
In this expanse, the joy just flew.

From black holes to bright novas bright,
Each sound weaved a colorful sight.
The universe hummed a cheery song,
In this night, all were joyful and strong.

Lightyears of Lyrics

Wormholes opened with a cheer,
As aliens danced, enjoying beer.
They belted out songs from afar,
While meteors played the bazoo guitar.

Venus turned with a wink and a flip,
As Mars tried to join in with a quip.
Gargantuan roars of laughter thrived,
In this raucous night, all felt alive.

Singing about love from the void,
Tiny asteroids all overjoyed.
Lyrics flew from star to star,
Some were odd, but that's who we are.

A sonic boom echoed, people yelled,
Across the cosmos, joy was held.
With each note, the universe spun,
In every heart, there was pure fun.

Astronomical Soundscapes

In a nebula, echoes gleamed,
Laughter rippled, as if it dreamed.
Singing Saturn slung notes so high,
While asteroids danced, passing by.

Galaxies twinkled with friendly flair,
Constellations twirling without a care.
A symphony played, oh what a show,
Even black holes joined in the flow.

From superclusters to mere dust,
Everyone knew that to sing was a must.
Together they laughed and spun around,
In this realm, true joy was found.

With comets zipping, the night felt right,
All creatures joined in with pure delight.
As stars serenaded the vast unknown,
They sang of love, with laughter grown.

Galactic Groove

In the depths of space, all stars align,
Planets join in, sipping on moonshine.
A comet cuts in with a flashy dance,
While aliens laugh—who gives them a chance?

A rocketship band plays a wild tune,
As asteroids bounce under the light of the moon.
Nebulas twirl in a shimmering haze,
Outer space parties, now that's just class A!

Echoes in the Void

In the realm where silence meets the beat,
Asteroids bob, tapping their tiny feet.
A neutron star hums a jazzy refrain,
While black holes chuckle, harboring no pain.

Warp speed whispers, they giggle and cheer,
While time bends over, it can't help but leer.
Voices collide, like comets on track,
And echoes bounce back, never holding back.

Sunbeam Symphonies

Solar flares play like trumpets on high,
Radiant rays waltzing through the sky.
Planets sway in a glittery trance,
Flares leading a luminescent dance.

Sunspots grin with a shimmering flair,
Making melodies, spreading joy everywhere.
Lightyears apart, yet we all can sing,
With laughter that echoes, what joy it brings!

Luna's Lullaby

The moon chimes in with a whimsical tune,
While the stars all wink under the watchful dune.
Crickets join in with a chirp and a peep,
As cosmic critters shake off their sleep.

Shooting stars twinkle like pixie dust,
In this galactic jamboree, sing we must.
Luna rolls her eyes, but she can't resist,
This cosmic cabaret, it tops the list!

A Symphony of Spacetime.

In the void, a mic was found,
Aliens gathered round and bound.
Singing tunes from light-years back,
A rubber duck was on the track.

Flying whales plucked notes from stars,
While Martians strummed on candy bars.
Their voices echoed, strange and grand,
As they rocked across the barren land.

Through black holes they belted high,
Comets danced to the lead guitar ply.
Saturn's rings jingled in delight,
As Uranus joined with a giggle and fright.

So here's to space, the bizarre night,
With hiccuping ghosts, it's a true delight!
Join the fun with a laugh so bright,
Together we'll sing 'til morning light!

Celestial Serenades

Under the glow of a distant sun,
Martian legends have just begun.
Jupiter's moons tap their feet,
While Venus serves up drinks, oh so sweet!

With asteroids spinning a wild bass,
And space cows hoofing at a lively pace.
A galactic band played tunes so weird,
Even black holes cheered, no one feared!

Nebulae twinkled like disco balls,
While space mice danced through cosmic halls.
Aliens rocked in shimmering shades,
As laughter echoed through starry glades.

In this cosmos, where all is bright,
We're here to party till the first light.
So grab a comet, don't be shy,
Let's sing and jump and reach for the sky!

Interstellar Harmonies

A cat on Mars sang a jazz tune,
While Pluto grooved by the light of the moon.
Asteroids played a trumpet so bold,
Filling the ether with stories untold.

Space pirates danced on solar sails,
Telling jokes of their salty tales.
While stars winked from a proper height,
In a galaxy where wrong feels right.

A comet zoomed with a shiny grin,
Giving space bears a chance to spin.
As meteors fell with glittering spark,
They sang of love in the endless dark.

So tune your ear to the cosmic beat,
Together we'll frolic on starlit street.
Where laughter rings through the vast expanse,
And every world joins in the dance!

Melody Among the Stars.

In a galaxy far, with a twisty fate,
Dancing aliens couldn't wait.
Belting tunes that made stars laugh,
Even comets turned up for the gaff.

A saxophone played from a nearby pod,
While cosmic cats gave a little nod.
The robots malfunctioned, but who cares?
They joined in raps, throwing up their gears!

Orbiting planets jived in sync,
As a meteor hitched a ride to the brink.
Quasars flickered while shooting stars glowed,
Turning this night into a special ode.

So, raise your voice to the endless skies,
Sing loud and proud, let your spirit rise!
In this stellar romp, our hearts take flight,
Together we thrive on this galactic night!

Celestial Jukebox

The stars throw a party, oh what a sight,
Planets are grooving, dancing all night.
Asteroids tapping their tiny feet,
Comets are swirling to the catchy beat.

In the back, the black holes sing songs,
Their voices echo, where nothing belongs.
Saturn's rings play a jazzy tune,
While Mars strums softly on a green bassoon.

Galaxies spin like they're on a spree,
Neon bright in cosmic glee.
Uranus chuckles, it's feeling quite bold,
As he hits the notes, the stories unfold.

With each little twinkle, the night goes on,
Even space dust joins, humming a song.
The universe giggles, in playful delight,
Under a spotlight of shimmering light.

Astral Duet

Two stars are belting a duet sincere,
Humming along as the asteroids cheer.
Mars harmonizes with a soft, smooth tone,
While Venus tosses in a glimmering drone.

Saturn spins tales of dancing rings,
Jupiter laughs as he joyfully sings.
Pluto, the odd one, bags a solo fame,
Though he complains no one remembers his name.

Space whales wail in a chorus of fun,
Echoing laughter through light-years won.
Stardust rains down with a sparkly flair,
Filling the void with musical air.

Together they sway in the velvet night,
Creating a magic, a wondrous sight.
The universe claps, in perfect rhythm,
As they take a bow, in cosmic symbiosis.

Rhythms of the Nebula

In the fog of colors, a beat starts to glow,
The nebula dances, putting on a show.
Nebulous twirls under the moon's watchful eye,
While the stardust shimmies, floating nearby.

Shooting stars zip as they join in the fun,
Chasing the meteors, a stellar run.
The Milky Way struts with a bass line profound,
While dancing quasars spin round and round.

Echoes of laughter ripple through space,
As each little star finds its own happy place.
Constellations wink, they know all the moves,
Together they frolic with rhythmic grooves.

As planets collide in a humorous clash,
The universe giggles at each funny bash.
The night fills with joy, the cosmos unite,
In a whirl of delight, oh what a sight!

Cosmic Crescendo

A melody rises from the depths of the night,
Galactic symphonies take off in flight.
Orion strums a celestial guitar,
As starry notes shimmer, near and far.

The comets join in, with tails all ablaze,
Singing of laughter through a cosmic maze.
Black holes hum softly, in rhythm and rhyme,
While supernovae crash, a spectacle sublime.

The constellations shift in a playful dance,
Spinning and twirling, caught up in the trance.
Neptune's bubbles pop in a jolly old tune,
As laughter floats softly past the great moon.

As the night reaches peak, a crescendo so grand,
Even dark matter waves, lending a hand.
The universe grins, a fun-loving spree,
Under the spotlight of infinity.

Futuristic Fugues

In a place where aliens dance,
Singing silly songs in a trance,
With tentacles twirling left and right,
They crack jokes under starlit light.

A robot jumps in with a beat,
Clanking metal feet, oh so fleet,
With glitchy voice, it starts to rap,
While space cows moo and do a clap.

Holo-screens flash, the rhythm sways,
Pizza's delivered to the space bays,
Each high note creates a rainbow burst,
Then all the comets queue for their first.

As laughter echoes through the void,
Each tune a joyfully sung avoidance,
Aliens take turns on the stage,
In this fun-filled celestial cage.

Voices of the Void

Echoes bounce in the empty dark,
Where a purple blob strikes a quirky spark,
It croons out tunes with a lumpy sound,
As meteors begin to whirl around.

A space whale joins with a gentle puff,
Adding depth, though it's rather tough,
To keep on key when you've got no lips,
Just blowholes and a few cosmic quips.

Stars twinkle along to the beat,
While asteroids dance on floating feet,
Quasars wiggle, trying to chime,
Making up words that don't even rhyme.

Out there, in this vastness so odd,
Singing with pride, like a cosmic god,
In the expanse, these voices collide,
Creating laughter as they collide.

Galactic Singularity

In a vortex of laughter, we drift and glide,
Silly sounds shake as we take a ride,
A comet sings high while a black hole groans,
Lost in the music, we dance like drones.

With each quirky tune, planets will sway,
While sardonic suns make bright melodies play,
A light-year journey, packed with gags,
As solar winds carry our joyful brags.

Raiding asteroids with beats so loud,
Space critters gather, forming a crowd,
They laugh and twirl, unaccustomed to fun,
In this galactic show, they've finally won.

The grand finale? A wormhole twist,
Singing in ways that defy an artist,
Galaxies burst with emotional flair,
As we laugh ourselves silly, floating in air.

Melodious Exploration

In the depths of space, a tune ignites,
As satellites swirl in a dance of lights,
With goofy lyrics on alien tongues,
They belt out tunes as the universe hums.

With lasers strumming a funky beat,
All the moons start to bob their feet,
Pluto jokes about being so small,
We cheer him on, "You're the best of all!"

Jupiter's competing, singing loud,
While Saturn twirls in its bubbly shroud,
An interstellar showdown of glee,
As even black holes join in with a 'whee!'

Together we weave a song of delight,
In this strange place, where everything's bright,
With laughter as fuel, we voyage afar,
Exploring the cosmos, our own shining star.

Echoes between Galaxies

Stars twinkle in the void, they sway,
Planets hum tunes, in their own way.
Aliens drop beats, they're ready to sing,
While comets jam out, their tails a fling.

One black hole spins, it's a dancefloor tight,
Alien DJs mix beats through the night.
Space whales sing low, creating a show,
Asteroids clap, making rhythms flow.

Astro-turtles moonwalk, they glide and groove,
Lunar bunnies hop, they've got the moves.
While Martians throw jokes, like confetti in air,
The Milky Way hums with a whimsical flair.

In this stellar cabaret, it's all in good fun,
As light-years fade out, we're not yet done.
With a wink and a laugh, they strut their stuff,
In the vast universe, we can't get enough.

Ethereal Echoes

Nebulae swirl in a colorful mist,
As stardust beings can't help but twist.
Saturn's rings shine, a disco ball bright,
While shooting stars dance into the night.

Giant frogs croak tunes from a blue gas ring,
Moon mice scurry, and they start to sing.
Jupiter rumbles with a beat so loud,
As all cosmic critters gather the crowd.

In the quiet of space, echoes erupt,
With laughter and joy, they all interrupt.
Uranus jokes about his tilted spin,
And laughter erupts from deep within.

At this celestial party, no one feels shy,
As they wave their antennas, reaching for the sky.
With every soft note, they connect as one,
Making ripples in space, until they're done.

Harmonies of Light

Light beams frolic with joyful fizzes,
Wormholes shimmer with confusing blizzes.
Orbs of color chatter, amusingly loud,
As they sing songs to the curious crowd.

Fluffy cloud creatures float on soft notes,
While solar sails dance like joyful boats.
Galactic caterwauls mix with glee,
At this whimsical jam from light-years free.

Whirling round planets, their voices soar,
Silly space shenanigans you won't ignore.
While echoes of laughter bounce through the void,
Every ounce of joy is meticulously deployed.

A fantastical circle where no one feels blue,
With a wink and a grin, they're singing for you.
In this vibrant expanse, let your spirit take flight,
As melodies sparkle through the fabric of night.

Silhouettes in Song

In shadows of starlight, figures sway,
As silhouettes laugh in a cosmic ballet.
Space pandas groove with their bamboo delight,
While green men hum tunes that tickle the night.

Old satellites twist in an orbiting spin,
Echoing rhythms that rattle within.
When meteors crash, they add to the beat,
In this charming assemblage, where joy is sweet.

Comets wear shades, looking oh so cool,
As funky spacecraft rev up, ready to rule.
Dodging stardust, they twirl and dive,
With this grand ensemble, the galaxy thrives.

In this jovial rave, all are welcome here,
Every sound, every laugh, brings us near.
So grab your space partner, and don't be shy,
Under the vast dome, let spirits fly high.

Astral Melodies

In a galaxy far and wide,
Aliens tap their feet with pride,
Singing tunes to planetary beats,
With Martians shaking their greenish treats.

Stars twinkle like disco lights,
As comets dance on satellite nights,
Saturn's rings join in a spin,
While Jupiter hums with a goofy grin.

Neptune strums a space guitar,
While pink space whales float by afar,
The Milky Way is the stage tonight,
With all the aliens feeling just right.

Planets take turns on the mic,
Pluto's raps are not what you'd like,
But laughter fills the cosmic space,
As they sing and dance, a merry chase.

Sounds of the Solar Wind

The solar wind whips up a cheer,
As asteroids join for a drink and beer,
Rockets zip past, they can't quite find,
The rhythm of the universe, one of a kind.

Uranus has the quirkiest tunes,
While Venus flirts under vibrant moons,
Mars beats on a rock for the show,
With giggles echoing, both fast and slow.

Astro-dogs spin in cosmic ballet,
Shooting stars come out to play,
With each note, comets laugh and glide,
In this wacky space where dreams reside.

Black holes pull in all the fun,
While Neptunians dance, oh what a run!
Together they sing through vast night skies,
In a whirlpool of joy, a sweet surprise.

Vibrations of the Void

In the void where silence reigns,
Comets hum and rocket trains,
Stars collaborate in wiggly jigs,
With disco balls made of moonlit twigs.

Neon meteors in a flash,
While photons bounce with a vibrant thrash,
Aliens shout, 'Bring out the sound!',
As space cats prance all around.

Gravity pulls a funky groove,
While satellites sway and start to move,
Laughing black holes create a beat,
As the universe dances, oh so sweet.

In a swirl of colors, planets blend,
Singing harmonies that never end,
With giggles and joy, they slip and slide,
In a carnival of the stars, they take pride.

Shooting Star Sing-Along

Shooting stars race across the night,
With radiant trails that shimmer bright,
Galactic choirs join to sing,
Of alien crushes and interstellar bling.

Planets stretch in a joyful pose,
Saturn dips and Jupiter knows,
A chorus of laughter fills the space,
As Earth brings cookies to the race.

In nebulae, the colors play,
While cosmic winds just sway and sway,
Aliens toast with fizzy cheer,
To the celestial tunes that we hold dear.

As the Milky Way spins a tale,
Of starry love that will not fail,
Celestial bodies sing along,
In this cosmic party, where all belong.

Starlit Serenade

Under twinkling lights we sing,
Aliens join in, what a fling!
A Martian tunes his rubber band,
While dancing dust bunnies take a stand.

Space cows moo in perfect pitch,
As comets weave and do a stitch.
Neon asteroids hop and sway,
In this galactic cabaret!

Planets spin, but don't lose grace,
Hammering stars bring heartfelt bass.
Saturn's rings are tambourines,
While shooting stars jump in between.

Laughter echoes through the night,
As black holes twinkle, what a sight!
Jupiter groans, "give me some room,"
As we sing 'til the sun finds bloom.

Celestial Chords

Eclipsed by laughter, we all cheer,
Galaxy's got nothing to fear.
An octopus plays a kazoo,
In this space show, we're all brand new.

Venus strums an old guitar,
While stars tap dance from afar.
Comets bark and sing along,
Making sure we can't go wrong.

Asteroids crash in perfect time,
Pluto sips on sparkling slime.
We joke of gravity's tight grip,
As everyone takes another trip.

Planets bounce with cosmic cheer,
Let this moment last, my dear!
With one last note, we fade away,
Reaching for another day.

Melodies of the Milky Way

Under the stars, we raise a toast,
To the oddest voices, we love most.
A purple snail sings pop all night,
While meteorites take flight with delight.

The stars make pies, oh what a treat!
Singing recipes with a funky beat.
Galactic poodles bark in glee,
As Saturn spins a mystery.

Laser beams create a tune,
As frogs on Venus croon at noon.
Black holes whirl like a dance floor,
Making sure we always want more.

A chorus of laughter fills the sky,
While space whales bubble—oh, my!
With every laugh, eternity sings,
In this universe, we touch the strings.

Interstellar Harmonies

Stars align for a grand old show,
Uranus brings the disco glow.
A robot sings an off-key verse,
While galaxies burst in a joyful hearse.

Supernovas pop with zest,
Jupiter jumps, it's the best fest!
A comet dips to catch the beat,
As orbits sway in rhythmic feet.

Neptune's bubbles add some flair,
And moonlit fireflies fill the air.
We trade our voices, laugh and shout,
In the great unknown, there's no doubt.

With rocket ships as our best friends,
The laughter echoes, never ends.
As we spin in this grand galore,
In the universe, always want more!

Cosmic Cadence

In a galaxy far, they sing out of tune,
Stars stumble around under a bright cartoon.
Planets spin wildly, lost in the beat,
While comets throw shade from their seats.

Martians dance silly with disco ball hats,
Uranus plays bass while Venus sings chats.
Space cows join in with a moo and a twirl,
As Saturn rings their bells with a swirl.

Neon asteroids throw glitter in the air,
While space dust settles on a rockin' chair.
Aliens giggle, exchanging a glance,
As black holes dance in a whimsical trance.

With moonbeams lifting the spirits so high,
Shooting stars serve snacks with a wink and a sigh.
Laughter erupts, it's a cosmic delight,
As they all sing out into the deep night!

Nebulae Refrains

In the swirls of gas, voices take flight,
Galactic gigs that sparkle so bright.
Spaceships park close to enjoy the show,
As gravity waves dance and sway to the flow.

Neon jellyfish float to the sound,
While time travelers jump up and down.
Celestial beings with harmonies rare,
Share giggles and joy in the shimmering air.

Constellations clash in a jazzy parade,
With each twinkling note, another mistake made.
But who needs rhythm in the great void of space?
When every wrong note finds a perfect place.

Meteor showers rain music on high,
While planets strum strings with a wink of an eye.
The universe chuckles, a raucous affair,
So let's sing together, with laughter to share!

Starlight Serenade

Under the glow of the flickering stars,
Intergalactic crew jamming in cars.
With each quirky note, a supernova pops,
And the space-time fabric joyfully flops.

Sirius strums chords from a radiant seat,
While earthlings provide an offbeat retreat.
Neptune brings snacks in bubbles of blue,
And all of the cosmos joins in for a chew.

A quasar croons in a voice that's so bold,
While black holes swallow every note told.
Laughter erupts as notes spin and spin,
Because who cares if the rhythm's not in?

With suns that dance and asteroids glide,
The melody travels on a playful ride.
As stardust showers from above like a spell,
They laugh, sing, and wish for the night to dwell!

Astronomical Acapella

Gather 'round, a celestial choir,
With plucky notes that reach even higher.
Orion's belt becomes a mic stand,
As meteors fall, lending a hand.

Galaxies swirl in a ludicrous blend,
With alien antics they happily send.
The Moon cracks jokes while Saturn rolls its eyes,
As laughter bursts free with each funny surprise.

Supernovae sparkle, pumping up the groove,
While asteroids do a funky little move.
Mars joins in with a chipper little tune,
While Pluto, shy, hums a catchy cartoon.

So let's belt out notes with a galactic shout,
Through the vastness of space, we'll twist and we'll flout.

With each twinkle above, we'll sing very loud,
In our quaint little corner, we're proud of our crowd!

Galactic Chorus

In a nebula, they gathered bright,
Planets swayed to a wild delight.
Asteroids danced in silly spins,
While comets howled their outlandish grins.

Stars flashed with neon shades,
As black holes twirled in grand parades.
Moonbeams chuckled, lost in rhyme,
Jupiter's giggles echoed through time.

Uranus flipped with a cheeky jest,
As Saturn's rings spun like a fest.
Aliens crooned their own bizarre tunes,
Sipping stardust from cosmic spoons.

The Milky Way joined the raucous cheer,
With quasar beats that drew us near.
Galaxies hummed the night away,
Cracking jokes in their stellar display.

Starlit Stage

On a stage made of sparkling light,
The sun took the mic, ready to ignite.
A chorus of stars sang off-key,
While meteors jived, so wild and free.

Planets tried their best dance moves,
But gravity gave some an awkward groove.
Martian missed a cue, took a fall,
As lavas erupted, causing a ball.

Venus laughed, shining bright and bold,
Telling stories of love never told.
With each laugh and giggle, the night grew,
Creating memories in outer view.

Black holes spun a funky tale,
With echoes of stars that danced without fail.
The universe wobbled in harmony tight,
Bringing joy to this galactic night.

Singing with Satellites

Satellites swayed, tuned to the sound,
Whirling in orbits, spinning around.
They belted tunes in a pixel parade,
As asteroids clapped and planets swayed.

With garbled voices, they tried a ballad,
Even Mars joined in with a goofy salad.
The moon spun tales of cheese so fine,
While stars winked, a glittery vine.

In unity, they crafted a beat,
While cosmic mics shimmered in the heat.
Each verse more silly, they giggled away,
Echoing laughter 'til the break of day.

As the space tunes danced through the night,
They harmonized under meteorite light.
With joy abundant and emissions bright,
This was a show that broke the starlit night.

Universal Notes

Notes drifted across the starry sea,
Quantized laughter, wild and free.
Bouncing rhythms from black hole's core,
While quasars beamed, asking for more.

Lost in tones of the vast unknown,
Where even the dwarf stars called their own.
Galaxies misjudged a high-pitched cheer,
Unexpected solos made the cosmos leer.

Sirius cracked a joke about time,
And Andromeda joined with a chime.
With dust clouds swirling and laughter spun,
Intergalactic happiness had begun.

Together they forged a harmony bright,
Delivering joy through the endless night.
In the symphony of the skies above,
They laughed and sang, radiating love.

Cosmic Chorus Call

In the void, the stars do sing,
Aliens dance, and bluebirds swing.
Asteroids tap their little feet,
While comets join in for a treat.

Neon lights blink in delight,
Galaxies spin, oh what a sight!
Planets spin their tales so grand,
As space whales croon across the land.

Fuzzy hats on Martians wear,
While black holes puff out smoky air.
Saturn's rings twist like a bow,
A chorus of laughter's what we sow.

Shooting stars in sparkly suits,
Jive with moons in sequined boots.
Every meteor makes a splash,
In this concert, we all bash!

Radiant Riffs

Galactic guitars strum away,
With zero-gravity ballet.
Neon Nebulas groove and sway,
Under light of the Milky Way.

Starships zoom with vibrant flair,
While aliens play without a care.
A cosmic drumroll, loud and neat,
While space-time dances to its beat.

Wormholes twist, a dizzy treat,
Planets rumble, can't be beat!
With cosmic claps and swirling fun,
The universe shines, they've just begun!

In the ether, laughter flows,
With every note, the joy just grows.
Radiant riffs in twilight bloom,
As starlight fills the empty room.

Harmony Among the Stars

In a nebula, the music's bright,
Stars line up in pure delight.
Aliens chant in cosmic cheer,
While asteroids bop without a fear.

Aquatic planets play on slides,
Mars brings snacks for fun-filled rides.
Around the rings, the laughter flies,
As karaoke echoes, oh, how it sighs!

Twirling comets lead the pack,
While space giraffes dance in slack.
Every note a joyful fling,
As creatures join the cosmic swing.

Harmony sings in vibrant hues,
While planets toast with colorful brews.
A festival of joyful sounds,
Among the stars, where bliss abounds.

Aetherial Anthems

Shooting stars bring harmony near,
While cosmic critters cheer and jeer.
In a space bar, they share the thrill,
With intergalactic jokes to spill.

Martians rhyme with solar flair,
As light-years fly through starry air.
In this realm of upbeat tunes,
No one cares for the afternoon.

With flashy lights and alien hugs,
The Milky Way pulls dance floor plugs.
Asteroids tap their tiny toes,
As cosmic laughter freely flows.

Galaxies form a joyous scene,
Bouncing rhythms so serene.
In this place of laughs and dreams,
Aetherial anthems burst at the seams!

Phosphorescent Phantoms

In the glow of stars so bright,
Ghosts grooving, what a sight.
With a wink and a twirl, they sway,
As black holes hum the night away.

Asteroids tap their rocky feet,
Comets join the cosmic beat.
Nebulae swirl in colors bold,
Their laughter echoes, tales retold.

Planets giggle in their orbits round,
While Saturn's rings make the best sound.
Shooting stars wish with glee,
Join the jam, come dance with me!

In this wild galactic spree,
Phantoms sing of infinity.
A waltz with aliens, oh what fun,
Under the watch of a glowing sun.

Ethereal Harmony

In a space where time stands still,
Whimsical notes give a thrill.
Uranus plays the bass guitar,
While Venus strums near and far.

Aliens laugh with every tone,
Creating melodies of their own.
Jupiter's thunder, a beat so grand,
With Martians tapping, hand in hand.

Galaxies twirl, a dancy delight,
Their bright lights flicker, what a sight!
Singing memories of years gone past,
Echoes of laughter, a spell they cast.

In this realm of singing stars,
The universe strums its guitars.
Twinkle and shine, in perfect cheer,
Join this gig, the night is near!

Song of the Celestial Bodies

Orbs collide in rhythmic play,
Melodies float in a witty way.
Meteor showers, a wild refrain,
As supernovas burst, not in vain!

Rocket wails with a fizzling sound,
While space dust dances around.
Cosmic crooners all take turn,
Singing loud of what they yearn.

In celestial bars where starlight beams,
The frolic of planets fuels wild dreams.
Black holes hum, a jazzy tune,
While comets glide by, a colorful swoon.

Eclipses sway in the moonlight's glow,
Dancing shadows steal the show.
In this concert, laughter's the key,
Join our song, come dance with me!

Whispers of the Universe

In a nook where the comets chatter,
Galactic giggles, what's the matter?
With stardust sprinkled on their hats,
The whispers float, no need for spats.

Twinkling jokes that never tire,
Space otters dance around the fire.
With a twirl and a playful spin,
They sing of where the fun begins.

Pulsars pulse to the rhythm fine,
While meteors race, a playful line.
Laughter echoes through the skies,
As galaxies wink with knowing eyes.

In this space, where time feels light,
Whispers bring pure delight.
Join the band, don't be shy,
Let's serenade the stars up high!

Radiant Resonance

In a galaxy far, far away,
Aliens sing their songs all day.
With a twinkle and a boom,
They dance inside their room.

A Martian croons in offbeat tones,
While Saturn's rings make funny groans.
Each note floats on stardust breeze,
As laughter echoes through the trees.

The comet spins and joins the fun,
While Pluto tries to join, but runs.
They harmonize in silly prance,
In spacesuits, they all dance.

Galactic giggles fill the void,
As aliens make a joyful noise.
With every belch and every sneeze,
The universe sways with utmost ease.

Cosmic Refrain

Starlight shines, a tweak in tone,
And Jupiter's tune is overblown.
With a kazoo and a boom box,
They belch out laughter like a fox.

Venus winks as she starts to sing,
And Nebulas flock to join the fling.
A wobble here, a jiggle there,
While asteroids twirl without a care.

Dance around a black hole's rim,
To a rhythm that's funky and grim.
Sirius stars proudly sway,
While comets leap and then decay.

With laughter that twinkles in the night,
The cosmos hums in sheer delight.
Each note is silly, bright as day,
As the galaxies join in to play.

Melodies Woven in Light

Shooting stars twirl like dancers bold,
As rambunctious space cats sing of old.
With glitter scattered everywhere,
They spin their tales without a care.

A nebula bursts with colorful cheer,
While meteorites throw in a sneer.
The rhythm climbs and flutters high,
As space whales sing to the sky.

In rings of gas, they twist and shout,
A raucous song, there's no doubt.
With cosmic giggles and silly flair,
They forget all troubles in the air.

Oh, what a night, with beats so bright,
As friends from afar illuminate the night.
These tunes of mischief, bounce, and play,
In a universe, where laughter is the way.

Intergalactic Harmonies

Far beyond the Milky Way,
Monkeys swing and start to play.
They grab a mic, start to bellow,
While planets spin as merry fellows.

Uranus giggles, what a sight,
As it shakes to the left and right.
Martians clap, full of delight,
Making sure the mood is light.

Galaxies hum a goofy tune,
As asteroids dance around the moon.
With twinkling stars that flash and dive,
The universe feels so alive!

With every note, they share a grin,
In this party, nobody can win.
But laughter floats from star to star,
As joyous moments stretch afar.

Harmonies Across the Heavens

Stars twinkle, jiving in space,
A comet sings with a smiling face.
Planets laugh in a silly tune,
While moons spin round like a disco ball's swoon.

Galaxies doing the cha-cha slide,
With Jupiter hosting, oh what a ride!
Saturn's rings shine like dance floor lights,
While Mars throws shade, joining the sights.

Neptune's deep voice, deep as the sea,
Bubbles of laughter float wild and free.
A symphony of giggles from afar,
As shooting stars join in, what a bizarre!

In a dance of orbits, the universe plays,
With spacetime bending in rhythmic displays.
So grab your mic, let your inner star shine,
In this joyous realm, all voices align.

Echoes in the Ether

Sirius howls like a dog in glee,
While Orions's belt becomes a VIP.
Comets chalk lines in a cosmic trace,
As nebulae groove in a colorful space.

Black holes swirl with a mystic tune,
Inviting all beings to join this festoon.
Aliens cha-cha with intergalactic grace,
As they wiggle and jiggle in the vast open place.

Time bends and twirls like a ballerina,
While quasars shout, 'Hey, check out our arena!'
The echoes of laughter bounce off the stars,
As they chat with a wink from Jupiter to Mars.

An asteroid belt taps its rocky feet,
As meteors burst in a rhythmic beat.
So let's join this quirky cosmic affair,
For in the ether, joy fills the air.

Celestial Crescendos

Venus hums a whimsical whine,
Kites of starlight weave and entwine.
Meteor shower, a fireworks display,
With all the planets ready to sway.

Uranus makes a fart with a grin,
While Earth spins a tale of how we begin.
With laughter ricocheting through the dark,
Even black holes chuckle, creating a spark.

A symphony forms in the vast expanse,
As dust bunnies join in the dance.
The universe sings; it's silly yet grand,
As galaxies twirl, united and spanned.

Here's to the notes of absurdity bright,
In the cosmic play, each star takes flight.
With harmonies ticking like clocks, what a show,
In this vastness, we let our light grow!

Music of the Milky Way

Waves of sound ripple through starlit streams,
Quasars giggle, exploding like dreams.
The sky's a canvas, splashed with delight,
As aliens clink glasses on a wild night.

Asteroids shimmy with a clunky beat,
While moons do the moonwalk, oh what a feat!
The solar winds whisper tunes soft and low,
As Nebulae twirl, putting on a show.

With every note, suddenly we're all friends,
Dancing through shadows, where laughter transcends.
Constellations play games of hide and seek,
And the pulse of the universe creates a mystique.

So come join the frivolity up in the skies,
Where cosmic laughter and melody rise.
In this symphony of the great and the small,
Let the music of the galaxies embrace us all.

Harmonious Horizons

The stars are tuned to a brand new song,
Planets dance, but they don't belong.
Aliens jam with a zany beat,
Even comets stomp their feet.

Nebulas spin, colors make you grin,
Singing fish swim where the laughs begin.
Galactic giggles echo in the void,
Who knew space could be this absurdly enjoyed?

Meteor showers rain with glee,
Shooting stars wishing to be free.
With every strum of a space guitar,
Life on Earth feels less bizarre.

So let's sway in the Milky Way's embrace,
As laughter lights up this endless space.
In the universe's chorus, we find our place,
Beaming joy from a celestial base.

Starlit Improvisations

Under the glow of a moonlit smile,
Silly aliens croon in a dazzling style.
Singing in tongues, they bellow and screech,
Making a ruckus, a curious speech.

The sun winks down, caught in the groove,
Jupiter's twerking; it's a cosmic move!
Saturn's rings spin in offbeat fashion,
Creating a rhythm that sparks the passion.

With every bounce, the asteroids sway,
Dancing to tunes that nobody plays.
Planetary parties where gravity may bend,
As each note soared, the laughter won't end.

Orion's mutable belt jingles along,
As we've perfected an interstellar song.
Even black holes can't pull us away,
When starry tunes easily play!

Celestial Singers

A chorus of stars ignites the night,
With shimmering voices that feel just right.
Galaxies flaring in colorful hues,
Making music out of cosmic blues.

Asteroids juggling, with jokes in their folds,
While Martians dance in their fanciest golds.
A stellar choir of hiccups and cheers,
As laughter travels for light years and years.

Shooting stars cry out with laughter and cheer,
While Pluto insists it's still up for a beer.
Wormholes twist with hints of a jest,
Every note delivered with humor and zest.

So raise a toast to the solar delights,
For magic lives in the strangest sights.
In this vast space where the fun never lingers,
We'll jam with the joyful celestial singers.

Astral Requiem

In shadows of night, a playful tune,
Dancing through dust of a midnight dune.
The stars are chuckling, their glimmering jest,
As they hold a circus in each tiny quest.

Clumsy moons wobble in sparkly shoes,
Fumbling their notes, but they can't lose.
Comets whistle while dodging the grind,
A melody crafted for just the unwind.

Quasars giggle in bursts of bright light,
While supernovas blast, setting everything right.
With each twinkling jest, laughter's the theme,
Even black holes spin, caught in the dream.

So let's raise our glasses to this joyous spree,
For fun is the spirit of the galaxy!
With echoes of laughter across the night sky,
Let's sing this astral requiem high!

Harmonies in Gravity

In the sky, stars sing a tune,
Planets dance, under the moonlight's boon.
Saturn's rings twirl like a merry band,
While comets waltz, oh isn't life grand!

Jupiter's voice booms, a bass so deep,
While Mars tries to rap, but it's hard to keep.
Venus croons softly, sweet as can be,
Together they laugh, in a galactic spree.

Black holes are DJs, spinning the platters,
With nebulae lighting up like mad hatters.
Stars giggle and twinkle, a shining delight,
This gravity party, oh what a sight!

Uranus just jests, with jokes from afar,
While Pluto quips, "I'm a planet—what are you, a star?"
With laughter unbound, they drink in the void,
Music of the spheres, never to be toyed.

Cosmic Chords

Strumming on stardust, the Milky Way's path,
Every note echoes, inciting a laugh.
Galaxies spin with a laughably swish,
Creating a harmony, oh what a wish!

Neptune plays keys on a shimmering cloud,
Jupiter's drums, play boisterous and loud.
Everyone gathers for a stellar dance,
In this quirky concert, all get a chance.

Supernova sparkles, each burst a delight,
Spinning in circles, they whirl through the night.
Aliens bop to a beat never found,
In this silly soundscape, fun knows no bounds!

Lyrics made of light, laughter and cheer,
With echoes of joy ringing through the sphere.
As quarks and leptons cheer from afar,
We sing with the cosmos, our favorite bazaar!

Cosmic Jukebox

Step right up to the starry booth,
Select your track, let loose the truth.
Sing with the meteorites, tap with the moons,
Dance to the melodies of hapless raccoons.

Asteroids slide in, shake their rough edges,
Bopping along to whimsical pledges.
Each chorus erupts like a supernova,
In this neon-lit nebula, pure euphoria!

Uranus croons songs of the awkward and bold,
While Mercury jests, and the sun laughs in gold.
Pluto's in the corner, sipping on rays,
While Venus enthralls in an elegant daze.

When the chorus hits hard, the comets collide,
With snickers and giggles, from side to side.
This jukebox of galaxies spins ever bright,
As we jam through the universe, into the night!

Melody Beyond the Moon

Beyond lunar valleys, where laughter resides,
The air pulses joyfully, on celestial tides.
Fanciful echoes from a brave little sprite,
Dance in the shadows of soft silver light.

Shooting stars Snapchat, in cryptic delight,
Whispering secrets on breezes of night.
With playful lyrics that tickle and tease,
They mock the black holes with riotous ease.

The moon hosts a talent, the spotlight aglow,
With jokes of the cosmos that steal the show.
While aliens giggle with snacks of stardust,
In this cosmic café, it's laughter we lust!

Melodies ripple, through space-time's embrace,
Creating a ruckus, a harmonious race.
Join in the mirth as we twist and we sway,
In the universe's concert, let's play and play!

Stellar Songbirds

In a nebula bar, the stars all align,
Singing off-key, but feeling just fine.
Planets sway gently, they tap with a beat,
While comets do the cha-cha, oh what a treat!

Galactic giggles fill the vibrant void,
A black hole laughs, but it's never destroyed.
Dancing in circles, with no cares in sight,
Twinkling together, they party all night!

Jupiter's jugglers throw moons in the air,
Saturn's ringed wonders spin, without a care.
The Martian mimes mime to laughter's great tune,
While Venus sings solos with a strange, bright swoon!

With sparkling juices poured from starry mugs,
The Milky Way troupe shares all of their hugs.
As stardust flows on, they don't miss a chance,
Each twinkling performance, a cosmic dance!

Space Dust Dances

Across the vast void, dust floats in the dark,
Each speck has a story, a one-liners' spark.
Fleecy and funny, they twirl with finesse,
As energy beams shimmer, causing lightness and mess.

Not one shy asteroid keeps its moves small,
They glide with precision, heedless of fall.
A meteor shower spills jokes into space,
With punchlines that twinkle, they fly with grace!

Nearby the wormhole, they spin like a top,
Side-splitting laughter, it won't ever stop.
With supernova bursts, they get a kick,
Each flash brings a chuckle—an interstellar trick!

As time stretches thin, they're lost in the cheer,
These tiny particles dance, year after year.
Fidgeting photons join in the delight,
Tilt your head back, and bask in the night!

Planetary Performances

Each planet takes turns at the center stage,
Mars tells a joke, fills the crowd with rage.
Mercury zips with a witty retort,
While Neptune just sighs, lost in a thought.

Earth does impressions of aliens in flight,
With giggles erupting, they bounce with delight.
Venus does ballet, a pirouette twist,
While Saturn forms rings, a sparkling fist!

Uranus, not shy, sings the blues with a grin,
With jokes about moons and the chaos within.
Pluto grumbles softly, counting his fans,
But who needs a crowd when you carry your plans?

Together they shine, these actors of fate,
No matter how far they'll appreciate.
The stage lights will twinkle, their laughter will rise,
As the universe chuckles, it's no surprise!

Night Sky Notations

With laughter like echoes from the twinkling stars,
They scribble their tales on celestial bars.
Constellations chuckle, with stories to share,
Each scribe in the sky has whimsical flair.

Orion's been working on his comic routine,
While Cassiopeia draws, a poetic machine.
The Little Dipper drinks cosmic coffee,
While Ursa Major glows, feeling quite lofty!

Shooting stars zoom with a wink and a grin,
Bestowing wishes for the hopeful within.
The sky is a stage, where the night has its say,
Bringing humor to life, in its own special way.

So gather around, let the laughter expand,
As the celestial chorus, a fun band.
At the pen of the night, with a laugh and a shout,
We'll write our own songs, 'til the sun comes about!

Chorus of the Cosmos

In a galaxy far, far away,
Aliens groove, they sway and play.
With tentacles twisting to the beat,
They move their feet in zero-gravity heat.

Singing tunes of a million suns,
Screaming laughter, who needs guns?
Moon rocks roll, join the fun,
Even black holes are on the run!

Planets spin in pure delight,
As space whales howl into the night.
Stars shine bright; what a sight,
Funky rhythms take their flight!

Each supernova drops a beat,
Saturn's rings can't help but cheat.
Galactic zingers, oh so clever,
In this jam, we're all forever!

Echoes in the Stars

Echoes bounce in the astral breeze,
Martians dance in polka-dot skis.
Venus sings a loveable tune,
Even Pluto wants to croon!

Satellites spin like disco balls,
Jupiter's tricky with his cosmic calls.
Light-years fly when we all start jiving,
Interstellar laughs, oh, we're thriving!

Comets crash with a playful cheer,
Sirius jokes, "I'm the star of the year!"
Galaxies twist with giddy grace,
Welcome to our timeless space!

Nebulae whirl, a dazzling slide,
Space pirates join, we take them for a ride.
Starlight giggles, the universe beams,
We dance like wild, chasing dreams!

Timbres of the Universe

Stringing laughter through the void,
Spheres of sound we've all enjoyed.
Nebulas hum and pulse with glee,
Waves of joy resonate in harmony.

Quasars blink with cheeky flair,
What's that? A meteor in mid-air!
Echoes of laughter scatter wide,
Space-time glitches, look – we've cried!

Harmonies from the core of stars,
Fueling friendships from Earth to Mars.
Dancing moons in funky clothes,
Can you hear how the universe glows?

Melodies rippling on solar wind,
Every note, a new friend pinned.
Jokes that fly faster than light,
Who knew starlight could be so bright?

Infinite Melodies

Stars are strumming on cosmic strings,
Laughter soars on giddy wings.
Gravity pulls them closer still,
Time wraps around, gives us a thrill.

Swooping asteroids, off-key slides,
Singing quirks the universe hides.
Eclipses dance to the outlandish beat,
Stardust swirls at everyone's feet.

Solar flares radiate like a joke,
While dust clouds puff up and poke.
Meteor showers rain down delight,
Who knew the cosmos could be so bright?

Each voice adds to the cosmic cheer,
Hubble bows, "Thank you for being here!"
In the vastness, a raucous blend,
Infinite tunes that never end!

Dances of the Nebula

Stars spin and twirl, what a sight,
Planets join in, feeling bright.
Asteroids waltz, oh what a thrill,
Singing the tunes of the galactic will.

Comets do the cha-cha with flair,
While black holes groove without a care.
Supernovae burst with a laugh,
As galaxies split up their math.

Each star in a dress made of light,
Jumps to the rhythm, pure delight.
They boogie and bounce through the void,
In this wild show, they're overjoyed.

So grab a partner, don't be shy,
Join in the fun beneath the sky.
Dance like it's your last chance to sway,
In this stellar ballet, come what may.

Sunlit Symphonies

Planets croon in a sunny key,
Singing of love and harmony.
Saturn's rings play the bass, so grand,
While Jupiter claps with a jovial hand.

Earth hums softly, a folksy tune,
While Venus twirls, light as a loon.
Mars drums beats with a rusty hand,
In this ballad of the solar band.

Asteroids bang on cosmic glass,
Making music that's bound to surpass.
While the sun's rays shine bright and clear,
Bringing laughter to all who hear.

So gather 'round, let's make a scene,
In the gallery of the serene.
Let's strum the stars till the break of noon,
Creating melodies to chase the moon.

Cosmic Echo Chamber

Whispers of stardust fill the air,
Echoes of laughter, hard to compare.
Astro-mice squeak in a playful rhyme,
While comets hum anthems sublime.

Galaxies cheer in a vibrant tone,
As spacetime wiggles, it's not alone.
Nebulae giggle, scattering light,
In this chamber of joy, all feels right.

Hitchhiker hitch, clapping their hands,
In this wild echo, everyone stands.
Singers of space in a celestial spree,
Making harmonious history, just wait and see.

With each twinkle, a note set free,
As aliens dance in jubilee.
So let's join the fun, no need for a plea,
In this echo chamber, just you and me.

Night Sky Harmony

Under the blanket of stars aglow,
Silly shadows dance, putting on a show.
The moon, a DJ, spinning the night,
As constellations groove in delight.

Shooting stars streak like flares of glee,
While the Milky Way sings an old memory.
Each nebula bursts with color so bright,
In the wacky ballet of cosmic flight.

Pulsars beat like a heart on fire,
While planets whirl, never tire.
With laughter that echoes through the vast dark,
Creating a symphony, a shimmering spark.

So dance with the cosmos, sway with jest,
In the night sky's harmony, simply the best.
Come join the fun beneath the heavenly dome,
In this galactic soirée, we're never alone.

Orbital Overtures

In the depths of space, they sing,
Stars in tow, let laughter ring.
Aliens groove with galactic glee,
While comets dance on a cosmic spree.

A toaster winks, it's got some flair,
And meteors burst in colorful air.
Planets sway to their own beats,
As moons join in with funky retreats.

Saturn's rings spin a tune so fine,
Jupiter jigs with a glass of wine.
Neptune howls, it's quite a sight,
As Venus twirls in sheer delight.

Sing it loud, oh stellar crew,
The universe is waiting for you!
With every note, the stars collide,
In this vast space where fun won't hide.

Sonorous Skies

Shooting stars become the stage,
As shooting stars release their rage.
The moon snickers, a cymbal crash,
While black holes spin in a jazzy smash.

Bubbles float with a pop and fizz,
Galaxies swirl, look how they whizz!
A sunbeam strums a playful tune,
While cosmic cats dance to the moon.

Echoing laughs in a starlit bar,
Time ticks slow, we've come so far.
Constellations, a radiant choir,
Singing tunes that never tire.

So grab a seat, join the blast,
For every moment's meant to last.
In this stellar night, we'll take a chance,
And let our spirits leap and prance.

Harmonizing with the Universe

Asteroids tapping their tiny feet,
While space whales sing a disco beat.
A nebula spins in a glitter swirl,
As everyone joins this galactic whirl.

Quasars blink to the rhythm divine,
While voices echo, a glass of wine.
Supernovae pop with a burst of cheer,
In this night where joy draws near.

Galactic sheep are counting stars,
While little green men strum guitars.
Shooting off jokes about light-years,
Filling the void with laughter and cheers.

So lift your glass, to the sky so grand,
Join in the fun, it's all unplanned.
As laughter echoes through cosmic routes,
We dance, we sing, no room for doubts.

Galactic Grooves

In a swirling galaxy, creatures sway,
Singing tunes that drift away.
A stardust DJ spins it right,
Mixing beats in the deep of night.

Black holes buzz with electric sound,
Stars twinkle, while dancers abound.
A medley of giggles and bubbly beats,
While planets clap their rhythmical feats.

With rockets zipping to the base,
Every being joins the race.
In this night, all doubt's erased,
As laughter overflows into space.

So let's unite in this stellar show,
Dance through space, let laughter flow.
In harmony, let's share the light,
As we groove beneath the cosmic night.

www.ingramcontent.com/pod-product-compliance
Lightning Source LLC
Chambersburg PA
CBHW072148200426
43209CB00051B/835